Happy Hamster

BY
MATHIJS
VAN DER
PAAUW

CHRONICLE BOOKS
SAN FRANCISCO

Who could ever
imagine that taking
care of such wonderful
creatures could evolve
into this book?

I dedicate this book
to all my hamsters,
past and present, and
the hopefully many in
the future!

Library of Congress Cataloging-in-Publication Data available.

ISBN: 978-0-8118-7114-3

Manufactured in China

Designed by Molly Baker
HamsterTracker.com

10 9 8 7 6 5 4 3 2 1

Chronicle Books LLC
680 Second Street
San Francisco, California 94107
www.chroniclebooks.com

Every effort has been made to present the information in this book in a clear, complete, and accurate manner; however, not every situation can be anticipated and there can be no substitute for common sense. It is important to use care and follow the exact recipe, as your hamster will eat anything you feed it. Too many fresh vegetables can be harmful for your hamster, so please save these recipes for special occasions. Check product labels to make sure that the ingredients you use are safe and nontoxic. Be careful when handling dangerous objects. The author and Chronicle Books hereby disclaim any and all liability resulting from injuries or damage caused during the preparation or consumption of the recipes in this book.

MAKE SURE ALL TOOLS AND VEGGIES ARE WASHED REALLY WELL BEFORE YOU BEGIN. AND DON'T FORGET TO WASH YOUR HANDS!

table of contents

introduction

Ever since I was a kid I wanted a hamster—preferably with a large cage and connected tubes all over the room. Years later, after reading many books about this wonderful creature, I finally decided to be responsible enough to take care of one. It was not long after the arrival of my first hamster, Jamy, that I started to ask myself questions: What does a hamster do at night when I am sleeping? How far can a hamster run on a treadmill?

By the time I got my second hamster, Julie, I was hooked. I started working on a system to try and track what these creatures were doing. Then I adopted my third hamster, Lucy. The name stuck. Today, a few hamsters later, Lucy 4.0 is the current star of my Web site.

My system keeps track of my hamster treadmill statistics; as well as publishing it in (semi) real time on HamsterTracker.com. Webcams are there too, although this is a bit silly—hamsters are nocturnal, and at night it's hard to shoot video. In the daytime a hamster sleeps (and this is not exciting video). I thought that it would be fun to run a Web site that automatically updates every hamster's move. Now, HamsterTracker.com is a photoblog of Lucy 4.0's adventures and activity.

It's been wonderful to experience how these things evolve! While having fun with my hamsters and bragging about it online, I made the now-legendary Hamster Plant recipe (see Flowers for Your Hamster on page 172). This easy and fun recipe was not only a treat for my hamster (and very enjoyable for me to observe), it generated so many great and positive reactions that it became the start of the "Cookin' 4 Lucy" series.

Who could ever have imagined that the book you are currently reading is a result of that?

It is my pleasure to share the following recipes, which you can share with your hamster(s). I hope you'll have as much fun cookin' and servin' these recipes as I did. And remember, feel free to experiment, but always make sure you are using hamster-safe food!

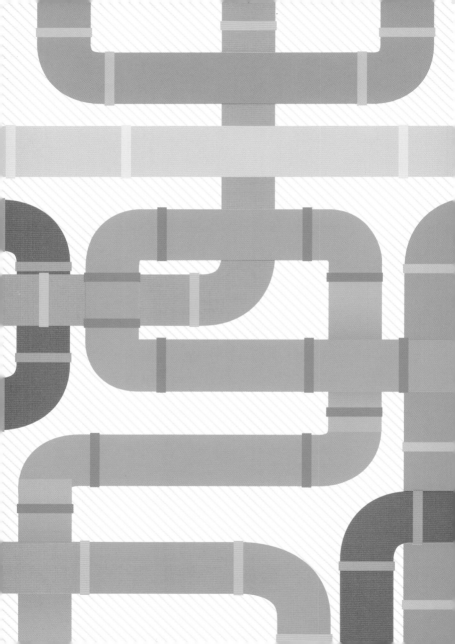

PANCAKES

Pancakes are truly universal. In the United States, they are preferred at breakfast, while in the Netherlands, they're an evening dish. There might even be a country where pancakes are enjoyed for lunch. Therefore, I present this all-time recipe to share with your hamster.

INGREDIENTS

Bread
Gouda cheese

TOOLS

Apple corer
Knife
Cheese slicer (or knife
   if you don't have one)
Microwave oven
Serving glass

STEP 1

Carefully cut out a pancake from some bread. Don't try to use Superman force—it doesn't work. Instead, gently twist the corer through the bread.

STEP 2

Repeat this three times. (You're an expert once you've finished).

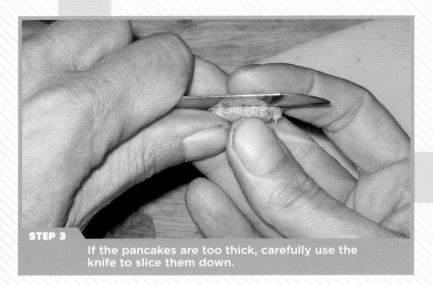

STEP 3

If the pancakes are too thick, carefully use the knife to slice them down.

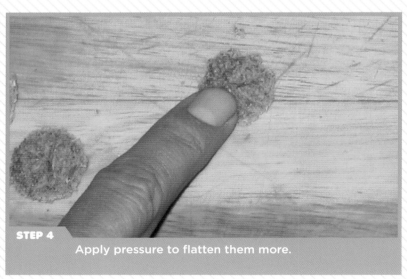

STEP 4

Apply pressure to flatten them more.

STEP 5

Carefully stack your pancakes.

STEP 6

Use the slicer to cut a thin slice of cheese.

STEP 7

Cut a square from your cheese slice. Then carefully cut out triangle shapes.

STEP 8

Use serious concentration with the last cuts, making a plus sign.

STEP 9

Admire your careful cutting!

STEP 10

Carefully lay the cheese on your pancake stack.

STEP 11

Microwave the stack for 5 seconds—just enough to melt the cheese slightly. (This step is optional.)

STEP 12

Beautiful!

I USED AN UPSIDE-DOWN WHISKEY GLASS AS A SERVIN' TABLE. THESE GLASSES HAVE GENERALLY A LARGER DIAMETER, AS WELL AS WEIGHT. I WOULDN'T WANT LUCY TO KNOCK THE THING OVER.

STEP 13

Place on a serving glass in your hamster's cage and wait.

dude, what's this? it smells great!

ULTRADRY CHICKEN SOUP

I started out by making chicken soup for myself. Then I realized that all the ingredients were there for me and Lucy to share.

INGREDIENTS

Small piece of boiled
   chicken
Carrot
Sweet red pepper
Zucchini

TOOLS

Serving glass

STEP 1

If making chicken soup for yourself, like I started out doing, cook 3 chicken legs in a broth for about 45 minutes.

STEP 2

Take the chicken legs out of the broth to cool down.

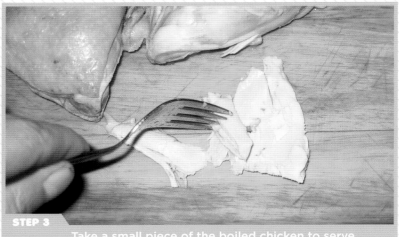

STEP 3

Take a small piece of the boiled chicken to serve your hamster.

STEP 4

Gather some hamster-safe veggies. I picked carrot, sweet red pepper, and zucchini. (I discarded the zucchini just before serving, since I wasn't completely sure it was hamster-safe.)

STEP 5

Put the veggies and chicken in your soup to cook for a few minutes. Meanwhile, proceed with hamster recipe.

STEP 6

Dice some of the chicken. Eat the rest you don't intend to feed to your hamster.

STEP 7

Stack on an upside-down serving glass. Hence the "ultradry" part of the name of this recipe.

STEP 8

Then just wait for your hamster to wake up. Which, for some reason (the smell), probably won't take long.

Lucy was a bit intimidated at first, this being her FIRST "Cookin' 4 Lucy" meal . . . So I served her a piece of boiled chicken, which she looooved.

HAVING HAD A TASTE OF THAT, IT DIDN'T TAKE LONG FOR LUCY TO EAT THE REST.

ULTRADRY CHICKEN SOUP

VERY NICE, DUDE . . . DID YOU COOK THAT YOURSELF?

♥ LUCY

CAN I HAVE SECONDS?

"It took Lucy only 69.59 seconds to pouch . . ."

—HamsterTracker

YOGURT IN A CUCUMBER BOWL

A nice and quick dessert for your hamster.

INGREDIENTS

Cucumber
Plain yogurt

TOOLS

Knife
Spoon

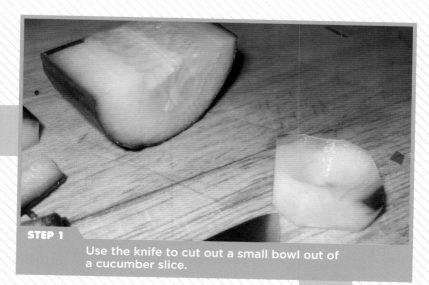

STEP 1

Use the knife to cut out a small bowl out of a cucumber slice.

STEP 2

Use the spoon to carefully fill it with yogurt.

STEP 3

Clean up the mess . . .

STEP 4

. . . and serve. Watch 'er go.

YOGURT IN A CUCUMBER BOWL

MMMM

Lucy didn't really like the yogurt, but she loved the cucumber!

She took a bite out of the side of the cucumber bowl, spilling yogurt all over her paws and cage.

(It was very funny to watch, I was too busy laughing to take more photos!)

I noticed that she took quite a while cleaning her paws, maybe secretly liking the taste of yogurt.

ANOTHER "COOKIN' 4 LUCY" WELL DONE!

R-ICE TEA

I cooked up this r-Ice Tea recipe after my vet mentioned it's good stuff for hamsters.

INGREDIENTS

Plain rice (not the fast-cookin' kind)
Water

TOOLS

Small pot
Timer
Drinking glass
Small bowl

STEP 1

Put 1/2 cup of rice with 2 cups of water in a small pot.

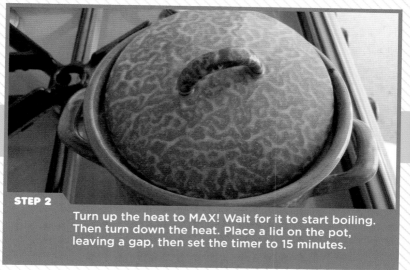

STEP 2

Turn up the heat to MAX! Wait for it to start boiling. Then turn down the heat. Place a lid on the pot, leaving a gap, then set the timer to 15 minutes.

STEP 3

After 15 minutes, drain the r-Ice Tea into a drinking glass.

STEP 4

R-Ice Tea and some cooked rice for your hamster!

Let the r-Ice Tea cool down for 10 to 15 minutes in the refrigerator.

Serve in a small bowl instead of the usual water bottle, since the bottle might be difficult to clean if used for liquids other than water.

CHEESY APPLE ROLLS

Here's an easy recipe when in a hurry.

INGREDIENTS

Slice of bread
Gouda cheese
Apple

TOOLS

Apple corer
Cheese slicer
Knife
Serving glass
Zip-top bag

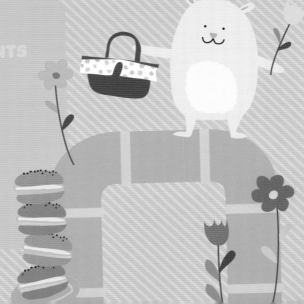

STEP 1

Using the corer, cut four small "rolls" from a slice of bread.

STEP 2

Using the slicer, carefully cut a slice of cheese.

STEP 3

Using the corer, cut out a circle from the cheese.

STEP 4

Using a knife, cut out a slice of apple and use the corer to cut out small circles.

STEP 5

Then stack the rolls on the serving glass and pack into the zip-top bag. Wait for your hamster to wake up . . .

STEP 6

. . . and wait . . .

THEN IT HAPPENED:

"We've NEVER seen Lucy
be this quick!"

—HamsterTracker

FRIED RICE

I simply love fried rice myself. Therefore I just had to come up with the following recipe, so that Lucy could have the same meal when I do.

INGREDIENTS

Cooked ham
Walnut
Cucumber
2 apples
Winter carrot
Cooked rice
   (see page 36)

TOOLS

Big knife
Small knife
Chopsticks (optional)

STEP 1

Roll the ham and, using the big knife, slice small slivers. If you like, eat the rest yourself.

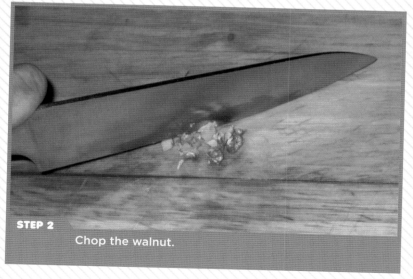

STEP 2

Chop the walnut.

STEP 3

Chop off some green from the cucumber.

STEP 4

Then slice the cucumber green into small bitties.

STEP 5

Remove the stems from the apples to make chopsticks for your hamster.

STEP 6

We want to add some apple to this recipe, too, so cut off a slice (before you eat the rest).

STEP 7

Dice the apple.

STEP 8

Using the small knife and a piece of winter carrot, design a bowl for the fried rice. I tried to design something fancy.

STEP 9

Outline looks nice!

STEP 10

Carefully cut out a bowl shape . . .

STEP 11

. . . which does require some patience.

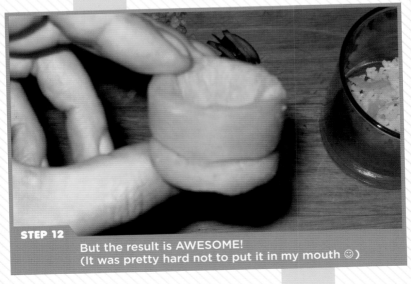

STEP 12

But the result is AWESOME!
(It was pretty hard not to put it in my mouth ☺)

STEP 13

Add the rice (and ham slivers).

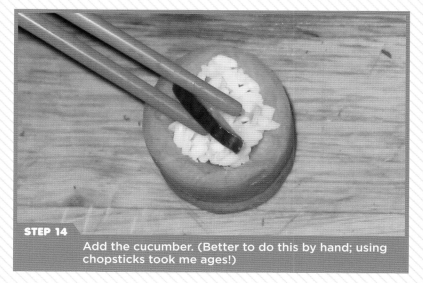

STEP 14

Add the cucumber. (Better to do this by hand; using chopsticks took me ages!)

STEP 15

ADMIRE!!!

STEP 16

Replace your chopsticks with your hamster's apple-stem pair.

"need this in my bedroom."

lucy

APPLE SUSHI

I had some sushi yesterday. While enjoying it, the following recipe came to mind, so now Lucy can enjoy some sushi, too.

INGREDIENTS

Apple
Cooked rice (see page 36)

TOOLS

Knife
Apple corer

STEP 1

Using the knife, cut a slice from the apple.

STEP 2

Admire the work you've done so far.

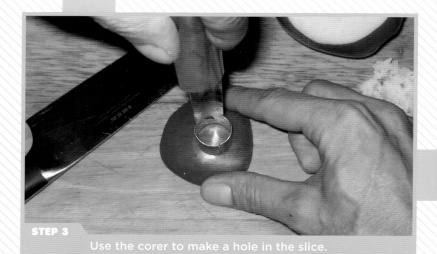

Use the corer to make a hole in the slice.

Admire again!

STEP 5

Cut the edges to make an apple cylinder.

STEP 6

The sun is for your own enjoyment!

STEP 7

Fill with the rice.

A CLOSE-UP

Please understand that this isn't even close to real sushi. It's inspired by real sushi. I love the real stuff *sooo* much, I needed to make a version for my hamster!

SAVIN' SOME
FOR LATER!

Another culinary
success!

BANANA-SPLIT CAKE

Always fun to make when feeling festive. All ingredients used can also make a perfect treat for you, as well as a wonderful cake for your hamster.

INGREDIENTS

Banana
Walnut
Soft-curd cheese
  (strawberry flavored)
Yogurt
Coconut shavings

TOOLS

Knife
Teaspoon

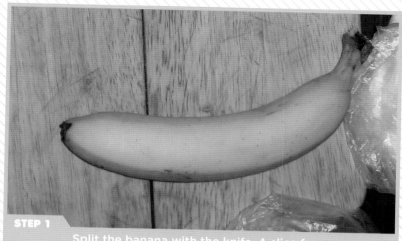

Split the banana with the knife. A slice for your hamster . . . and the rest for you!

Use a teaspoon to carve out a bowl from the banana.

STEP 3

Chop the walnut as finely as possible.

STEP 4

Add the soft-curd cheese.

STEP 5

Top it off with some chopped walnut.

STEP 6

ADMIRE!

STEP 7

Add some yogurt (as a whipped cream replacement).
Top it off with some coconut shavings.

STEP 8

Serve!

SERVIN' LUCY THE BANANA-SPLIT CAKE

"Mmmmm . . . this is new to me!"

VEGGIE TACOS

I thought it would be nice for Lucy to enjoy a veggie taco.

INGREDIENTS

Flour tortilla
Bag of chopped veggies
Gouda cheese

TOOLS

Wine glass
Knife
Cheese grater
Whiskey glass

STEP 1

Using the wine glass and knife, cut a circle out of the tortilla.

STEP 2

Using the same technique, cut another mini tortilla.

STEP 3

From the chopped vegetables select the following hamster-safe veggies: carrots, white cabbage, and bean sprouts.

STEP 4

Finely dice the white cabbage . . .

STEP 5

. . . and the carrot and bean sprouts.

STEP 6

Place on the mini tortillas.

STEP 7

Using the grater, grate some Gouda cheese.

STEP 8

Add a bit onto each taco.

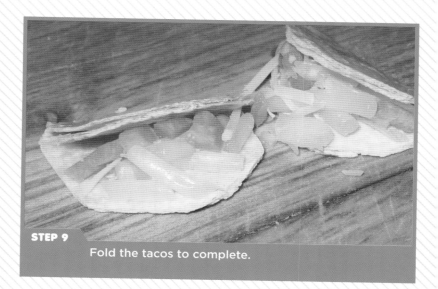

STEP 9

Fold the tacos to complete.

STEP 10

Use the whiskey glass as a serving table. TA-DA!

SERVIN' THE VEGGIE TACOS

"Great taste, dude!"

NOW LET'S HAVE A CLOSER LOOK!

CAN I REALLY HAVE BOTH?

VERY,

VERY

NICE!

NIBBL

It only took Lucy a couple of minutes to devour the first taco.

NIBBLE . . .

NIBBLE . . .

VEGGIE TACOS

DUDE, I WANT MORE!

THEN A SPLIT SECOND LATER:

"I'd love to have that again soon!"

MICRO VEGGIE PIZZA

It's always a good day for pizza!

INGREDIENTS

Flour tortilla
Carrot
Apple
Cucumber
Fresh parsley
Grated Gouda
Melon seeds
Pine nuts

TOOLS

Scissors
Drinking glass
Knife
Apple corer
Whiskey glass

STEP 1

Using scissors, cut open the tortilla bag.

STEP 2

Use the drinking glass as a cut-around guide. Using the knife, cut the tortilla.

STEP 3
Remove the cut-out tortilla. This will be our Veggie Pizza's crust.

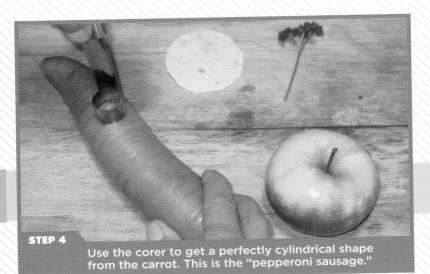

STEP 4
Use the corer to get a perfectly cylindrical shape from the carrot. This is the "pepperoni sausage."

STEP 5

Cut a few thin slices from the just-made "pepperoni."

STEP 6

Cut a V-shaped wedge from the reddest part of the apple.

STEP 7

Remove some of the apple—too much is too much.

STEP 8

Cut the apple into small blocks and carefully place them red-side up on top of the pizza.

STEP 9

Thinly slice some cucumber (leaving the green stuff on) and add to the pizza.

STEP 10

Top with some fresh parsley.

STEP 11

Add some Gouda.

STEP 12

Add 3 melon seeds (as "olives") and some pine nuts and place on the upside-down whiskey glass.

THE FINAL RESULT

Makes you kinda hungry, doesn't it?

SERVIN' LUCY THE MICRO VEGGIE PIZZA

"For ME???"

MICRO VEGGIE PIZZA

is there
anchovy
on this?

"DUNNO WHERE TO START HERE . . ."

I then explained to Lucy that she's not really supposed to eat all the ingredients from the top; she should take a bite from ALL of it!

VEGGIE HOT DOG

I thought it would be fun to cook a hot dog for my hamster.

INGREDIENTS

Bread
Carrot
Cheese

TOOLS

Scissors
Knife

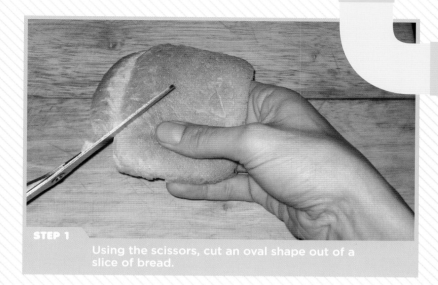

Using the scissors, cut an oval shape out of a slice of bread.

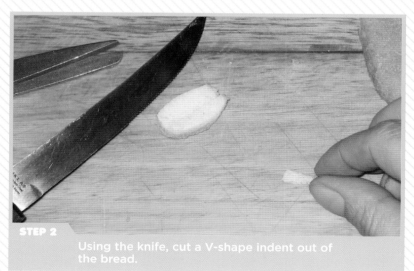

Using the knife, cut a V-shape indent out of the bread.

STEP 3

Cut a piece of carrot slightly longer than the bun you just made.

STEP 4

Place the "hot dog" on your "bun."

STEP 5

For mustard, use cheese. (Remember: Mustard is dangerous for hamsters!)

STEP 6

Cut out half of your "mustard" squiggle.

STEP 7

Cut out the other half.

STEP 8

Stack carefully, mimicking the wavy line of mustard.

SERVE ASAP, BECAUSE THE CHEESE CAN FALL OFF FAST WHEN PLACED ON THE CARROT.

CLUB SANDWICH

This is another personal favorite to have for lunch. While enjoying mine, this recipe popped into my mind.

INGREDIENTS

Bread
Gouda cheese
Winter carrot
Apple
Cucumber

TOOLS

Knife
Small can (washed)
Whiskey glass
Plastic bag

Using the knife, cut a 3-by-1-inch rectangle from a slice of bread. Flatten it using the small can. Divide it into three identical squares.

Add a slice of Gouda cheese to one of the squares.

STEP 3

Then add a slice of carrot.

STEP 4

Top it off with a bread layer.

STEP 5

Add a slice of apple. (Don't forget to wash it first.)

STEP 6

Cucumber is the next layer.

STEP 7

Add the last layer of bread and stick it all together with an apple stem.

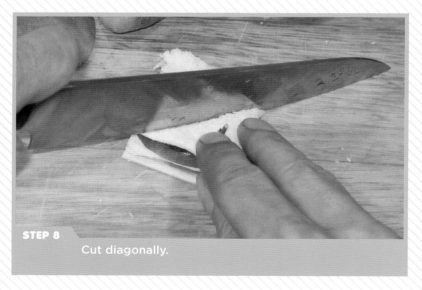

STEP 8

Cut diagonally.

STEP 9

Take a moment to admire your work and eat the part without the stem.

STEP 10

Place on the upside-down whiskey glass "serving table."

STEP 11

Wrap it in plastic while waiting for your hamster to wake up.

STEP 12

"Dude . . . I smell a Club Sandwich . . . Where is it?"

LUCY TOOK IT OFF
HER TABLE IN A SPLIT
SECOND ONCE SHE
FOUND IT.

no way am i gonna let this go!

MICRO BURGERS

I've been thinking about this for quite some time now. And I finally decided to give it a go. An apple corer makes the following recipe easier to create.

INGREDIENTS

Bread
Cooked ham
Gouda cheese (optional)
Fresh parsley

INGREDIENTS

Apple corer

STEP 1

Using the apple corer, cut out 2 round pieces of bread.

STEP 2

Do the same with a single (thinly) sliced piece of ham.

STEP 3

You can add some cheese if you desire Micro Cheeseburgers. Use the same coring method.

STEP 4

Place the ham "burger" and cheese on top of the bottom bun.

Use a bit of parsley (for the green stuff) and stack it all carefully.

STEP 6

Ready for serving!

SERVIN' A MICRO CHEESEBURGER

Lucy was extremely fast when she discovered her Micro Cheeseburger. Therefore, sadly, not all photographs are in focus . . .

Once Lucy noticed, she came runnin'.

This is a split second before she had a bite.

Who doesn't love hamburgers?

THIS IS
A SPLIT
SECOND
LATER!

YES!
LUCY
LOVES IT!

KETCHUP

LASAGNA

If you love lasagna as much as I do, and you also like to make it yourself, then this recipe is easy. You'll have all ingredients to make a version for your hamster, while yours is cooking in the oven.

AS I MENTIONED IN THE ULTRADRY CHICKEN SOUP RECIPE, I'M NOT COMPLETELY SURE ZUCCHINI IS HAMSTER-SAFE, SO PLEASE CHECK WITH YOUR LOCAL HAMSTER EXPERT.

INGREDIENTS

Lasagna noodle
Veggies (carrot, sweet red
    pepper, and zucchini)
Ham
Grated Gouda cheese

TOOLS

Knife
Servin' glass

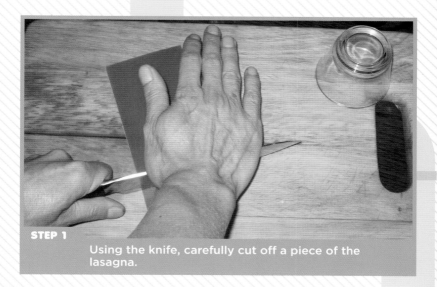

STEP 1

Using the knife, carefully cut off a piece of the lasagna.

STEP 2

As you can see, cutting straight isn't easy.

STEP 3
Dice the veggies. Cut a rectangle from a slice of ham and get the grated cheese ready.

STEP 4
Arrange the veggies in an artistic and rectangular shape on the upside-down serving glass.

Add some cheese and cut the lasagna into similarly sized rectangles (you'll need 2).

Stack carefully.

STEP 7

Add some more cheese.

STEP 8

And top it off with ham.

STEP 9

Carefully stack some more veggies.

STEP 10

Top off with cheese yet again.

STEP 11

If the previous step doesn't work for you (it didn't for me), downsize a little by removing the second layer of veggies.

STEP 12

Now the second layer of lasagna doesn't fall off!

STEP 13

Carefully place more veggies on top.

STEP 14

See if you can manage to top it off—it takes skill!

SERVIN' THE LASAGNE

"Dude . . . Have you been cookin' again?"

A CLOSE-UP

"Looks great!"

IT
TASTES
GREAT
TOO!!!

YUM

MMM!

SIMPLE PASTA

I enjoy my pasta so much that I had
to come up with a hamster version.

INGREDIENTS

Cooked and cooled pasta
Sweet red pepper
Parsley
Grated cheese

TOOLS

Whiskey glass
Knife

STEP 1

Place the pasta in a circle, thereby making a "bowl" of pasta on the top of an upside-down whiskey glass.

STEP 2

Using the knife, slice and dice the sweet red pepper.

STEP 3

Then add some parsley.

Don't forget some grated cheese to top it off!

THE SERVIN' OF THE SIMPLE PASTA DISH

"Smells Italian, dude!"

SIMPLE PASTA

JUUUUICE!

♥ LUCY

CAESAR SALAD

I was enjoying my own. Then this recipe struck me.

INGREDIENTS

Cucumber
Hard-boiled egg
Fresh parsley
Bread
Gouda cheese
Ham (optional)
Pine nuts

TOOLS

Knife
Teaspoon

STEP 1

Using the knife, cut off the thin end of a cucumber.

STEP 2

Then cut off a chunk at the bowl height for your hamster.

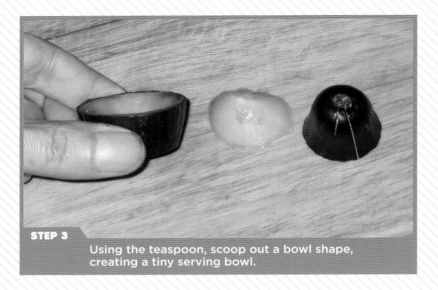

Using the teaspoon, scoop out a bowl shape, creating a tiny serving bowl.

Peel the egg and tear some parsley leaves into tiny pieces.

STEP 5

Toast a slice of bread, and cut a square from the middle. Slice the pieces in half (through the soft side) and then dice the halves, making croutons.

STEP 6

Put the parsley in the cucumber bowl.

STEP 7

Then add cheese, slice of egg, ham (if using), and croutons.

STEP 8

After adding 2 pine nuts, you're ready to serve!

DUUUUDE, IS
THAT FOR ME?

CAESAR SALAD

PLEASE TELL THE CHEF I LOVE THIS!

♥ LUCY

NOW WHERE SHOULD I PUT THIS?

EASTER EGG

I got this wonderful gift, from our close friend Dup, for Lucy and me to enjoy. When I asked for the recipe, she replied: "This is a really easy one . . ."

INGREDIENTS

Hard-boiled egg

TOOLS

Nontoxic paint
  (color of your choice)

STEP 1

Decorate the hard-boiled egg with nontoxic paint.

STEP 2

Peel off the shell from the top and cut out
a small piece for your hamster to nibble on.
(Enjoy the rest of the egg yourself.)

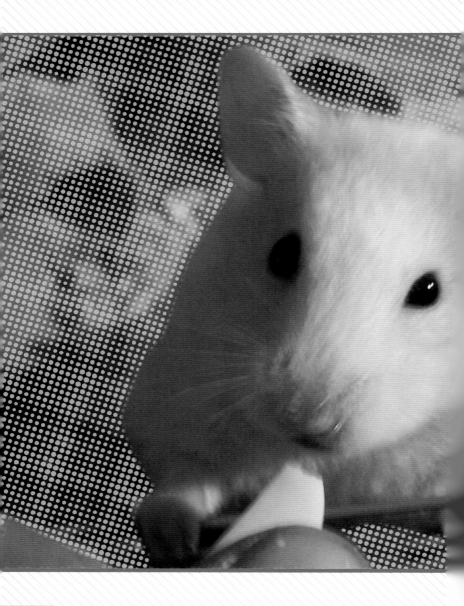

THANKSGIVING DINNER

When you're cooking the big meal for your loved ones, you shouldn't forget the petite among them. Even though turkey is the traditional Thanksgiving dish, Lucy and I prefer chicken, so that's what I've used for this special meal.

INGREDIENTS

Boiled chicken
Banana
Strawberry jam
Broccoli

TOOLS

Small knife
Toothpick
Scissors
Serving glass
Teaspoon
Small fork

STEP 1

Using the knife, cut a small piece of (cooled) chicken.

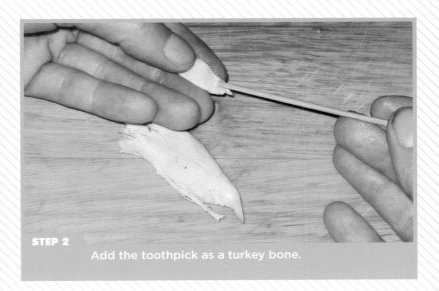

STEP 2

Add the toothpick as a turkey bone.

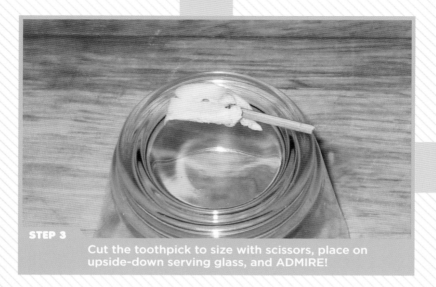

STEP 3

Cut the toothpick to size with scissors, place on upside-down serving glass, and ADMIRE!

STEP 4

For mashed potatoes, use a banana.

STEP 5

Mash the banana gently with the spoon.

STEP 6

Add your mashed banana to the dish.

STEP 7

Admire again!

STEP 8

For cranberries (which are poisonous to hamsters), use strawberry jam.

STEP 9

Add the jam to the dish.

STEP 10

Carefully make a cut near the top of a piece of broccoli.

STEP 11

This makes great hamster-size veggies.

STEP 12

Add the veggies to the dish.

Admire one last time before servin' it to your hamster.

VEGGIES —

FLOWERS FOR YOUR HAMSTER

Because you have to surprise your loved one once in a while . . .

A PLANT FOR LUCY'S CAGE

THE RECIPE IS SIMPLE:

1. Wash an apple and some fresh parsley.
2. Cut out a piece of the apple, preferably dice-shaped.
3. Use a toothpick to punch a small hole in the apple.
4. Place the parsley stem in the just-made hole.
5. Serve immediately!

**LUCY LOVED IT,
AS YOU CAN SEE!**

acknowle

The support, reactions, and suggestions, as well as friendships I made through the HamsterTracker.com community, makes my hobby of taking care of my hamster (and bragging about it online) so enjoyable. Thank you for the inspiration to keep on developing new recipes for your hamster to enjoy!

A special thank-you to Sarah, for all your HamsterTracker efforts!

dgments